Ferrari 33SP at Sebring

introduction

For over 100 years cars have dominated the world of transport. From very humble beginnings there are now an estimated 600 million cars worldwide. Whether it's to get to and from work or perhaps school, we all rely to a greater or lesser extent on the car, an international symbol of freedom.

A world reliant on the horse for transport was changed forever with the invention of the internal combustion engine – and particularly the four-stroke petrol engine unveiled in 1885 by two German engineers, Gottlieb Daimler and Karl Benz. Although that was over a century ago, the basics behind motor vehicle transport have remained the same. From standard cars to awesome world speed record breakers, they come in all shapes, sizes and powers.

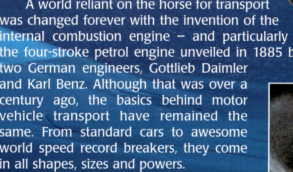
Elegance of yesteryear: Delahaye 135M

Dragster power

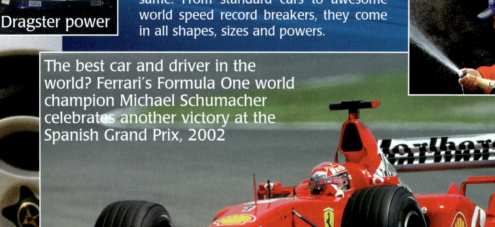
The best car and driver in the world? Ferrari's Formula One world champion Michael Schumacher celebrates another victory at the Spanish Grand Prix, 2002

The World land-speed record, held by Richard Noble in his jet-powered Thrust 2, stands at 633mph (1019kmh).

Early Renault

Model T Ford 1919

Citroën Traction Avant

motoring
milestone

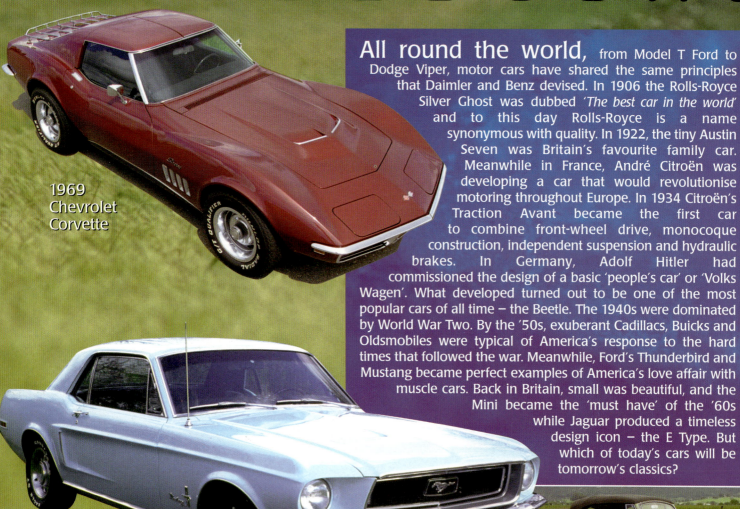

1969 Chevrolet Corvette

1968 Ford Mustang

VW Beetle

All round the world, from Model T Ford to Dodge Viper, motor cars have shared the same principles that Daimler and Benz devised. In 1906 the Rolls-Royce Silver Ghost was dubbed *'The best car in the world'* and to this day Rolls-Royce is a name synonymous with quality. In 1922, the tiny Austin Seven was Britain's favourite family car. Meanwhile in France, André Citroën was developing a car that would revolutionise motoring throughout Europe. In 1934 Citroën's Traction Avant became the first car to combine front-wheel drive, monocoque construction, independent suspension and hydraulic brakes. In Germany, Adolf Hitler had commissioned the design of a basic 'people's car' or 'Volks Wagen'. What developed turned out to be one of the most popular cars of all time – the Beetle. The 1940s were dominated by World War Two. By the '50s, exuberant Cadillacs, Buicks and Oldsmobiles were typical of America's response to the hard times that followed the war. Meanwhile, Ford's Thunderbird and Mustang became perfect examples of America's love affair with muscle cars. Back in Britain, small was beautiful, and the Mini became the 'must have' of the '60s while Jaguar produced a timeless design icon – the E Type. But which of today's cars will be tomorrow's classics?

AUTO info Over 15 million Model T Fords were sold between 1908 and 1927 when production ended

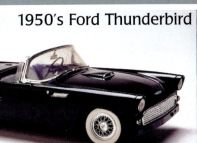
1950's Ford Thunderbird

Morris Minor Traveller

Morris Mini Minor

CLASSIC gallery

1922 Austin Seven

1930 Invicta 4.5-litre

Over the years cars have appeared on our roads in all shapes and sizes

E Type Jaguar

CAR DATA
Make: JAGUAR
Model: E Type
Engine: 3781cc
Horsepower: 265bhp
Top speed: 150mph (241kmh)
0-60mph: 7 secconds
Body: Streamlined 2-seater sports roadster

When building his first car, Henry Ford didn't realise it was too wide to fit through the workshop doors!

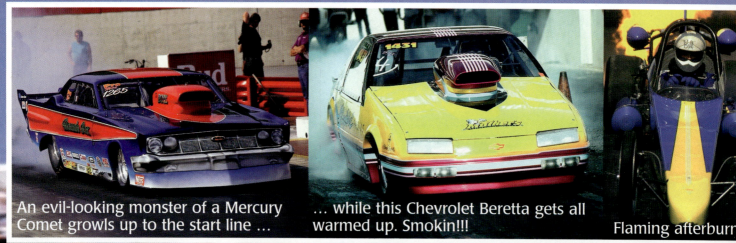

An evil-looking monster of a Mercury Comet growls up to the start line …

… while this Chevrolet Beretta gets all warmed up. Smokin!!!

Flaming afterburn

fast and furious

Obscured from the crowd by clouds of smoke, World Champion, Joe Amato (below), burns some rubber

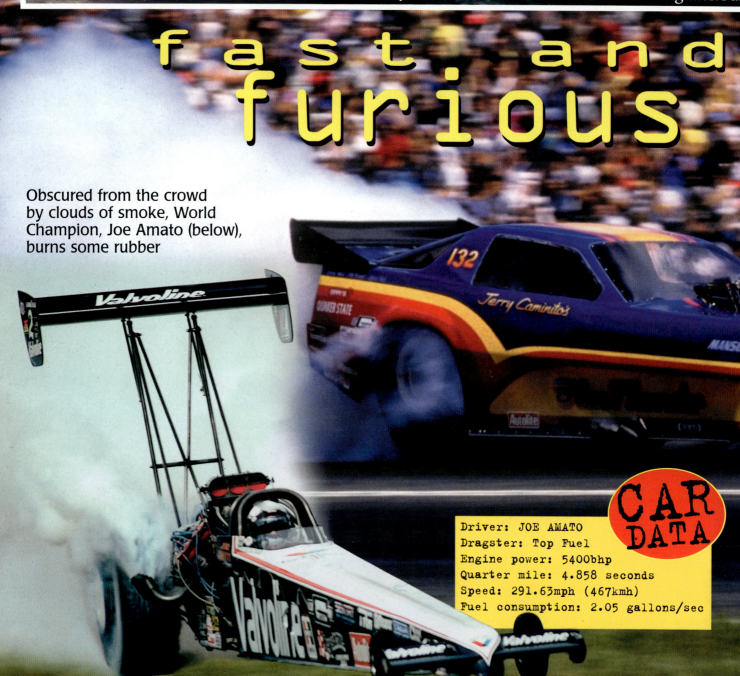

CAR DATA

Driver: JOE AMATO
Dragster: Top Fuel
Engine power: 5400bhp
Quarter mile: 4.858 seconds
Speed: 291.63mph (467kmh)
Fuel consumption: 2.05 gallons/sec

AUTO info One modern dragster has more power than 250 Model T Fords!

Legendary Corvette

Ford 'Pop' hot rod

Mega powerplant

DRAGSTER race-off

Drag racing is extremely popular, not just for the speed but also the spectacle of getting from A to B as loudly and quickly as possible. Started in America in the late 1940s by a group of 'hot rod' enthusiasts, drag racing has progressed from being an outlawed pastime to one of the most dramatic of motorsports.

The first races were run on roads outside towns between sets of traffic lights (along the main 'drag' hence the term drag racing). Never popular with the authorities, the racers were persuaded to move to disused airstrips and dry lake beds. By the mid-1970s drag racing had moved on to purpose-built race strips – now the fastest cars in the world could really go to war!

'Big Time' dragster

A **Funny Car** is based on a saloon car, but bears little resemblence to its showroom cousin. Using the same power plant as a Top Fueller, the engine is mounted in front of the driver.

A **Top Fueller** is everyone's image of a dragster. Big wheels at the rear, small wheels at the front, driver sitting in front of a huge engine. Capable of covering a standing quarter mile in 4.8 seconds at over 290mph (465kmh), these are the fastest accelerating cars in the world.

A blast of Canadian jet power

The drag race starting lights are affectionately known by enthusiasts as the 'Christmas Tree'.

1908 Austin Grand Prix car

A tight fit

Formula Junior crash, Thruxton, UK

single-sea
thrills

**DRIVERS RISK
LIFE AND LIMB
IN HI-TECH,
HI-OCTANE,
THRILL-FILLED
RACE CARS**

Saubers lead the pack during the Spanish Grand Prix 2002

At max power, engine valves open and close at a rate of 76,800 times a minute

Ready to race

Emerson Fittipaldi makes a pit stop at the Toronto Indy

Duelling Indycars

ACTION pix

At over seventy international venues from Formula One and Indycar circuits to NASCAR super-speedways, drivers compete in the most glamorous and passionate sport in the world. From the early 1900s, the world has been fascinated with speed and the thrill of watching men risking their lives in the pursuit of glory.

The first races were fought out on roads, but it was soon obvious that purpose-built tracks would be needed. The motor racing circuit was born and for the first time drivers were able to push their cars to the limit. From early heroes like Fangio and Moss, to modern legends like Senna and Schumacher the passion and excitement has continued.

Modern race cars are the result of years of research, testing and development on a par with the space and aircraft industries. When today's drivers squeeze into their cockpits they are sitting in some of the most advanced machines on the planet. Protected by a carbon fibre tub that is stronger than steel yet lighter than fibreglass, they drive these 900hp supercars round the racetracks at speeds in excess of 200mph. Aerodynamics and especially the use of front and rear wings aid the car's handling at these incredible speeds.

CAR DATA

Make: FERRARI
Driver: Michael Schumacher
Engine: 2998cc
Power: 900bhp
Top speed: 225mph (360kmh)
Body: Carbon-fibre

Drivers often experience as much as three times the force of gravity (3g) making high speed turns.

Refuelling a Porsche Carrera at the Daytona 24-hour race

Cockpit view

track stars

Austrian ace Karl Wendlinger above, drives his Audi TT-R to victory in Belgium

INCREDIBLE PERFORMANCE FROM THE WORLD'S SUPERCARS

Porsche 908 lines up ready for a 12-hour endurance race

Not all racing cars are open-wheeled single-seaters. In fact saloon car races in their many forms far outnumber the single-seat variety. At every level from the very physical battles of the stock car circuit to the élite of Le Mans, there is a whole kaleidoscope of cars competing to be first past the chequered flag.

While saloon cars are generally more aerodynamic than open-wheeled cars, they are also heavier. A NASCAR stock car, for example, is twice as heavy as a Formula One or Indycar. Despite this, saloon cars are still very fast – capable of over 200mph – and race almost exclusively on oval circuits where the cars get so close together that it is not unusual to see 30 cars racing nose to tail. High speed crashes are common, with multiple barrel rolls the spectacular result of a driver's error. A highlight of the NASCAR season in America is the Daytona 500. The Le Mans 24-hour is probably the most famous endurance road race in the world. Powerful supercars like the McLaren F1 and Jaguar XJ220 do battle along rural French roads which, for the rest of the year, are more accustomed to Peugeot 406s, Renault Clios and Citroën 2CVs.

Meanwhile, ordinary drivers can get a taste of motor racing by taking their own everyday car to a track day at a racing circuit. Here they will experience a little of what it is like to pit their skills against other drivers.

AUTO info Back in 1906, Renault won the first-ever Grand Prix motor race.

CRAZY! CAR BITS QUIZ

Check out these shots, they are all in *Car Crazy!* Can you find them and name the makes? If you get stuck, the answers are below, however, you will need a mirror to read them!

1 MG	2 Saubr	3 Morris	4 General Motors (GM)	5 Austin	6 Land Rover
7 Chevrolet	8 Ferrari	9 Citroen	10 VW	11 Lotus	12 Citroen
13 Ford	14 Chevrolet	15 Delahaye	16 Saubr	17 Ford	18 Bugatti
19 Alfa Romeo	20 Jaguar	21 Chrysler	22 Ford	23 Jeep	24 Renault

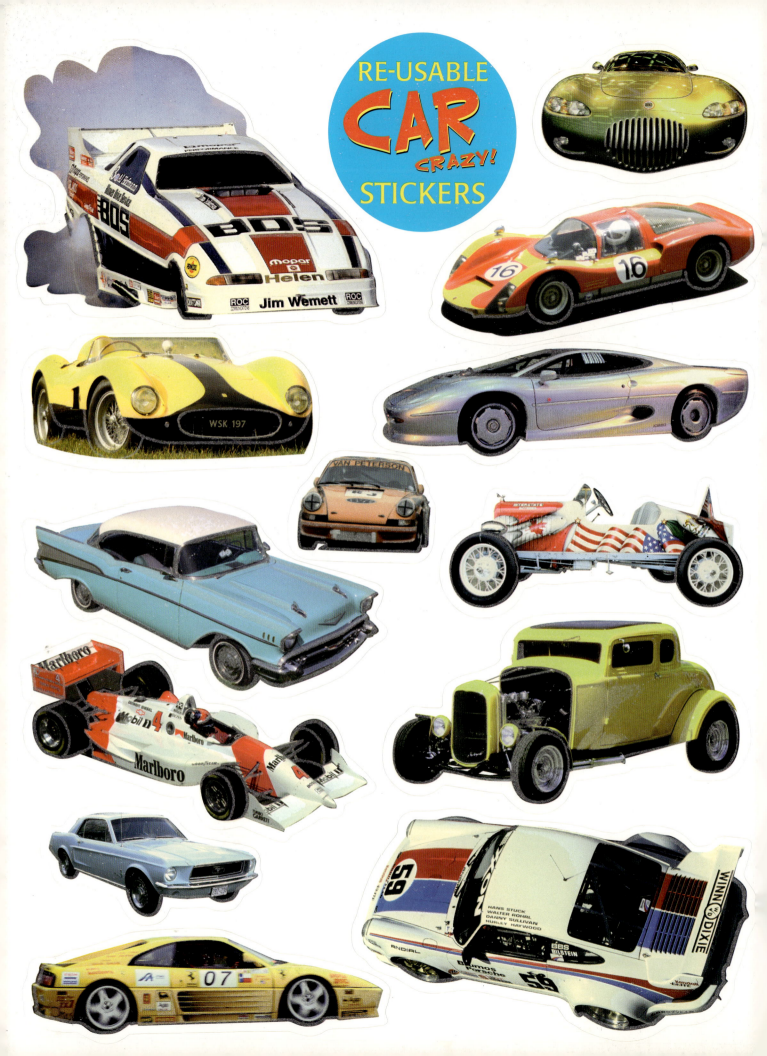

Oops! An early retirement for this NASCAR entry

Snaking round the Atlanta track

TRACKTION
gallery

```
Make:       PORSCHE
Model:      911 Carrera
Engine:     3.8 litre
Horsepower: 303bhp
0-60mph:    4.7 seconds
Top speed:  180mph (288kmh)
```

CAR DATA

Le Mans 24-hour starting grid

Porsche 911 on the racetrack

Open to almost anyone, Mexico's 1,864-mile Carrerra Panamericana, was the maddest road race ever!

Lotus GP type 25

SS 100 Jaguar

SPORTS
allstars

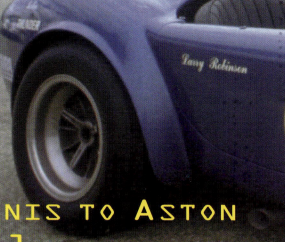

From Minis to Aston Martins, they race them all!

Porsche Carrera 6

AUTO info — The V6 engine in a Ferrari Dino was actually built by Fiat.

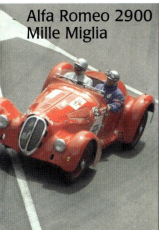
Alfa Romeo 2900 Mille Miglia

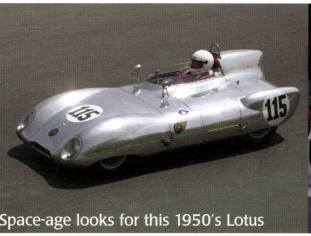
Space-age looks for this 1950's Lotus

Bugatti Type 35

sporting classics

Car racing has been popular for almost as long as the car itself has been on the road. Motorsport has evolved alongside the car with many examples of racing cars of yesteryear surviving to this day. However, not all historic racers have finished racing – not for them a cosy retirement in a museum. Some are still trackworthy and enthusiasts put these old racers through their paces, not holding back, but driving them as originally intended – to the limit! So, famous classics like MG, Jaguar, Bugatti and Porsche continue to record victories on the world's racetracks.

Austin Healey 3000Mk

CAR DATA
Name: AC SHELBY-COBRA MKII
Engine: 4735cc V-8
Horsepower: 300bhp
Top speed: 138mph (222kmh)
0-60mph: 5.6 seconds

At Le Mans, Ettore Bugatti once described the Bentleys as 'The world's fastest lorries'

Carlos Sainz's Toyota Corolla causes a dust storm in Africa

Phillippe Bugalski's Citroën Xsara WRC in Spain

dirt busters

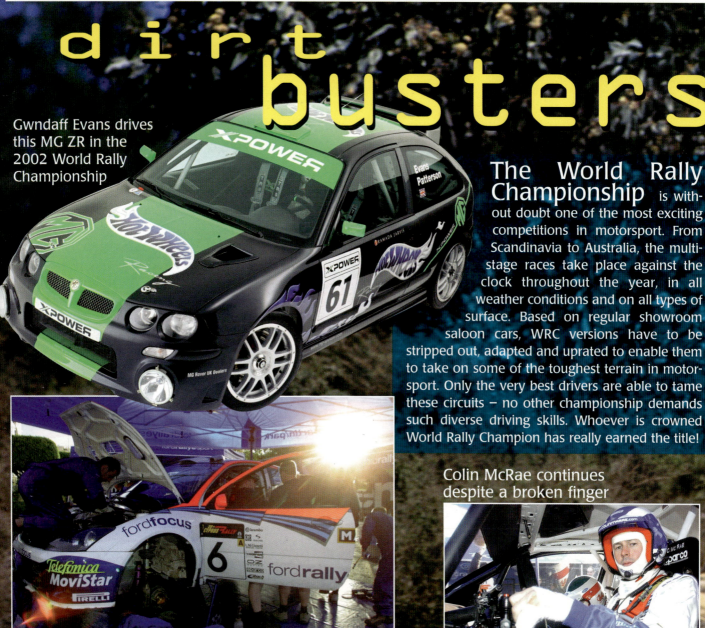

Gwndaff Evans drives this MG ZR in the 2002 World Rally Championship

The World Rally Championship is without doubt one of the most exciting competitions in motorsport. From Scandinavia to Australia, the multi-stage races take place against the clock throughout the year, in all weather conditions and on all types of surface. Based on regular showroom saloon cars, WRC versions have to be stripped out, adapted and uprated to enable them to take on some of the toughest terrain in motorsport. Only the very best drivers are able to tame these circuits – no other championship demands such diverse driving skills. Whoever is crowned World Rally Champion has really earned the title!

Night time is the only time for servicing

Colin McRae continues despite a broken finger

AUTO info The Skoda rally team has won more trophies than any other manufacturer.

Marcus Gronholm rides his Peugeot 206 around the Swedish Rally

Janne Paasonen's Mitsubishi Lancer in Cyprus

Colin McRae stays 'Focussed'!

RALLY gallery

SUPREME SKILL IS NEEDED WHEN YOU'RE AT THE WHEEL OF A RALLY CAR

Colin McRae drives his Subaru Impreza to victory in the 2001 Rally of Australia

CAR DATA

Make: SUBARU
Model: Impreza WRX
Engine: 1994cc
Top Speed: 143mph (230kph)
0-60: 5.9 seconds

After victories in the Alpine Rally, Lancia adopted an elephant emblem in recognition of Hannibal's!

Land Rover Discovery in the Camel Trophy

Tackling the Paris-Dakar Rally

let's off-road!

The latest craze in the motoring world is serious off-roading! From local tracks and fields to the most demanding endurance race of all – the Paris-Dakar Rally – four-wheel drive vehicles enjoy the unique ability to venture where no other cars can go.

The first 4x4s came from a military need, the Willys Jeep being a famous survivor of many a battle while, arriving in 1948, Land Rover has been the marque that has taken explorers to the most inaccessible and inhospitable parts of the planet – and returned them to the safety of civilisation!

Four-wheel drive means exactly that – power is sent to all four wheels of the car, instead of two wheel drive on conventional cars. The tough image of 4x4s has become popular with so many motorists, that lighter versions (or 'soft-roaders') are a familiar sight on high streets and motorways.

 Rover have experimented with using jet turbines to power some of their cars.

Land Rover Freelanders are funky 'go-anywhere' vehicles!

OFF-ROAD gallery

NOWHERE IS OFF LIMITS TO A 4×4!

CAR DATA

Make: LAND ROVER
Model: Series 3a
Engine: 3500cc V8
Body: All-terrain pick-up

Jeep Wrangler and (above) a wartime ancestor

The first multi-purpose vehicle (mpv) was a Willys Jeep Station Wagon back in 1946.

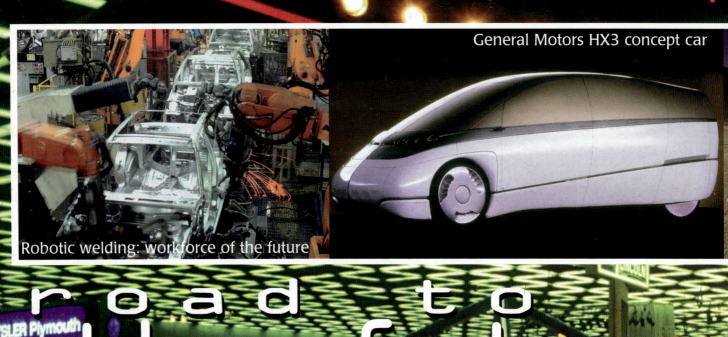

Robotic welding: workforce of the future

General Motors HX3 concept car

road to the future

Pontiac Protosport concept

Honda solar car

18

The longest road in the world is the Pan American highway ...